SECRETS
OF THE
SUPER ATHLETES

SOCCER

John Devaney

LAUREL-LEAF BOOKS bring together
under a single imprint outstanding
works of fiction and nonfiction particu-
larly suitable for young adult readers,
both in and out of the classroom.
Charles F. Reasoner, Professor of Ele-
mentary Education, New York University, is consultant to this series.

Published by
Dell Publishing Co., Inc.
1 Dag Hammarskjold Plaza
New York, New York 10017

Produced by Cloverdale Press, Inc.
Designed by Jon Dewey
Cover photo by Manny Millan/SPORTS
  ILLUSTRATED

Laurel-Leaf Library® TM 766734, Dell
Publishing Co., Inc.
ISBN 0-440-98399-1

Printed in the United States of America

First printing-June 1982

For the La Salle High School soccer team
and its coach

Acknowledgments

My thanks to Vince Casey, director of public
relations of the North American Soccer
League, for his help in gathering information for this book. Also most helpful were
the public relations directors of the New
York Cosmos, Chicago Sting, Tulsa
Roughnecks, Minnesota Kicks, Fort Lauderdale Strikers, and the Tampa Bay Rowdies.

Among many publications I found helpful were these: *The Official Soccer Book of
the United States Soccer Federation*, by
Walter Chyzowych; *A Thinking Man's
Guide to Pro Soccer*, by Gerald Eskenazi;
Learning Soccer with Pelé, by Pelé; *Winning Soccer*, by Al Miller; *Mastering Soccer*,
by Lowell Miller; *The Great American Soccer Book*, by Harvey Frommer; and Brian
Glanville's *A Book of Soccer*.

J.D.

PHOTO CREDITS

New York Cosmos: pp. 7, 30, 54, 56, 64, 71, 72, 74, 78, 81, 86, 88; Jann Zlotkin, courtesy of Fort Lauderdale Strikers: 10; Bill Smith, courtesy of Chicago Sting: 12, 32, 39, 41, 49, 93, 95; Rabbit Hare, courtesy of Tulsa Roughnecks: 16, 66; John Devaney: 19, 24, 25, 99, 103, 105; Barton L. Gilmore, courtesy of Fort Lauderdale Strikers: 43; Tula Roughnecks: 45, 82, 90; Ursula Timm, courtesy of Fort Lauderdale Strikers: 48; Richard Steinmetz, courtesy of Tampa Bay Rowdies: 51, 61; Judy Lotz, courtesy of Fort Lauderdale Strikers: 52; John Geders, courtesy of Tampa Bay Rowdies: 63; Thom Baur, courtesy of Fort Lauderdale Strikers: 68; Tampa Bay Rowdies: 80.

CONTENTS

INTRODUCTION

If you can kick a ball with the side of your foot, you are a soccer player.

Soccer has been called "the simplest game," for unlike football or basketball, there are no complicated plays. And unlike baseball, there are no special skills, such as hitting, fielding, and pitching, that you have to master.

However, there are mountains of books for the young athlete who wants to be a soccer player. There is much to learn and every player—rookie or superstar—must practice how to pass and how to score goals.

Goal! And Chinaglia celebrates. "Play to enjoy soccer," he says. "If you're not having fun, you won't play well."

Cosmos superstar Giorgio Chinaglia says, "Most of soccer is instinct. It is doing the right thing at the right time. It is seldom that you have the time to think and to remember what you were told to do. You just do it."

This book reveals what the pros do, and how they do it. These superstar secrets, which made them winners, will help you be a more skillful player and a more knowledgeable fan.

BEFORE
THE GAME

Giorgio Chinaglia, the high-scoring New York Cosmos star, walks slowly into the empty dressing room, the first to arrive for the game. But that's no surprise because Giorgio is *always* the first player to arrive for a Cosmos home game.

He sits on a stool in front of his locker and fishes out the rubber-cleated shoes he wears during a game. He pulls the leather laces off the shoes and carefully threads each shoe with new laces. Giorgio *always* wears new laces for a game.

Then, he pulls on the pair of blue-

and-white wrist bands he will wear for the first half of the game. He puts on a new pair for the second half. Giorgio *always* changes wrist bands after the first half of a game. "Yes," he says with a rueful smile, "I am just a little superstitious, yes I am."

Talent and skill are important to soccer superstars, but most players also believe in the power of luck. "The bigger the star," says Chicago Sting equipment manager Willy Steinmiller, "the more likely he is to be superstitious."

The most superstitious is Ferner, the West German goalkeeper. "I think you will find that is true on most teams," says the rangy, mustached Ferner. "You know why? Luck is important for a keeper. If a ball hits the post of the goal and bounds away, the keeper is a hero. If the ball hits the post and trickles into the cage, he's a bum. So to be good he's got to be lucky. And if you believe in good luck and bad luck, then of course you must be superstitious."

Ferner insists on wearing the same shin guards he's worn for the past nine years. "I have to glue them together before a game," says the Sting equipment manager. Just before a game Ferner asks an equipment man to place a towel on his back. He won't let anyone touch his shoes before a game. And he also demands that he be the last one out of the dressing room. "Sometimes," says the Sting's equipment manager, "one of the referees has to come down to the Sting

"Luck," say goalkeepers, "is a big part of goalkeeping." This goalkeeper for the Washington Diplomats is watching a little bit of luck come his way as the shot by Fort Lauderdale's Dave Hudson hits the post and bounds away.

dressing room and demand that Ferner come out so the game can begin.''

The Sting's high scorer, Karl-Heinz Granitza, is superstitious about his T-shirt. He wore the same T-shirt for every game during the 1981 season. ''I wore it because we kept on winning,'' says Granitza. ''I wore it right through to the Soccer Bowl.'' He'll wear it for the 1982 and 1983 seasons, he says, ''because we won the Soccer Bowl and the championship of the league so it must be a lucky T-shirt.''

''We had one player,'' says Willy Steinmiller, ''who always wore the same broken-down studs on his shoes, even though the studs can be easily replaced by screwing them off. He kept wearing those nubby studs until finally they broke off and he had to wear new ones. He said that the older his studs, the more goals he scored in a season.''

A star's superstitions can drive his coach up the locker room wall. ''I could never talk tactics or strategy to them before a game,'' says former California Surf coach Hubert Vogelsinger. ''They were thinking too much about their superstitions. I had some who would always put on their shoes first, then the rest of their uniform. There were other players who would put on their entire uniform except their pants, and they

The Sting's Karl-Heinz Granitza shouts to a teammate as he gets off a pass.

wouldn't put those on until just before the game. So they'd be running around before the game naked below their waists.

"When I'd say, 'OK, let's go out there and play,' there would always be a tremendous fight. There were always three or four guys who wanted to be the player who went out onto the field last."

No North American Soccer League team has more superstars than the Cosmos have and therefore they have more superstitious players than any team in the league. "It's true," says one Cosmos, "that the better the player, the more likely he is to be superstitious. It's like what the goalkeepers say: "Luck is important in scoring goals, and the more goals you score, the more you believe in luck."

When the team is on the road, Chinaglia always makes sure he sits in the same bus seat during the ride from their hotel to the stadium. "Once I forgot and sat in a different seat," Chinaglia says, his nut-brown eyes smoldering as he remembers. "We lost. I never made that mistake again."

Most Cosmos players drive to Giant Stadium in East Rutherford, New Jersey, for home games. "I live in New Jersey and it is not too far from the stadium," says the Cosmos goalkeeper, Hubert Birkenmeier. "But I always take the same route to the stadium. If I make a mistake and get on a new road, I go back to my house and I start over again. I make sure I get on the road I always take."

The team's best midfielder is "Bogey" Bogicevic. "He has a size 33 waist," says the Cosmos equipment manager, Charlie Kessel. "But he always wears double-X sized pants for the game. They are maybe four or five sizes too large. They really swing in the breeze."

Bogey simply tightens the drawstring on the shorts. "I like the pants to be baggy, you know," he says. "For me the baggier the shorts, the better my luck."

Worrying about their luck is only one part of the pre-game regimen for soccer superstars.

Most players think about their bodies. Others, like the Seattle Sounders' Steve Buttle, a midfielder, also think about their opponents. "I play with my head and not with my feet," he says.

"Soccer is a game of thinking as much as it is a game of running."

"Some stars believe that only the coach should worry about team strategy," says West German star Wolfgang Suhnholz, who once played for the California Surf. "The coach can't go out on the pitch with you once the game begins. Ten or 15 minutes before every game, I would sit alone. And I would think about the other team and the player I had to mark. I try to analyze how I can best play against them."

"I think about their forwards," says Cosmos goalkeeper Hubert Birkenmeier, "and I try to remember what foot they used when they kicked at me during penalty kicks or shootouts. You learn, after you've been a keeper for a while, that the good scorers will try to use the same foot in certain situations."

No matter how they get ready for a game, all soccer players have one thing in common—the tools of their trade—their gear. But not all the stars use those tools the same way. The regimen begins almost from the moment the player gets out of bed on the day of the game. The Sting's Arno Steffenhagen, an all-star midfielder, says, "I try to relax. I take a

Tulsa's Joe Morrone's (6) face shows the strain of a long game as a header goes by him.

walk. And I eat lightly, usually some kind of fish.''

Some prefer a heavy meal before a game. ''I put away a big steak three or four hours before a game," says Connecticut-born Joe Morrone, the NASL Rookie of the Year in 1981. He plays midfield for the Tulsa Roughnecks. "I like a good thick steak, as big as I can find, with a baked potato and a salad and a Coke. It's all settled by game time. And a thick steak will give you what you need most to play 90 minutes of soccer—endurance."

All players warm up with a variety of kicking and bending exercises. But a few, including "Bogey" Bogicevic and Morrone like to do their own kinds of stretching exercises, twisting themselves into the shapes of pretzels.

"The guys on the team give me flak about it and call me The Stretch Man," says Morrone. "But I feel that stretching exercises are the best for soccer because you want the muscles as loose as possible. You're going to do a lot of sudden sprinting and falling. If your muscles are not stretched, you can get hurt."

GEARING UP

"What hands are to a pianist," the legendary Pelé once said, "feet are to a soccer player."

The tender loving care of a soccer player's feet begins with his shoes. Most soccer superstars own three different types of shoes:

1. Flat-soled shoes for jogging before or after practice. A few players also wear these shoes when they play on artificial surfaces or "rugs."

2. Multi-studded shoes, most players use to play on the "rug." The studs are made of molded rubber or nylon and

18

most models have 14 to 16 studs. Giorgio Chanaglia and other players own two models of multi-studded shoes, a newer model with slightly longer studs. The longer studs work well on certain "rugs," the shorter studs on others.

A Sting player does a stretching exercise for the legs. His shoes are the flat-soled type worn for warming up.

3. Removable-studded shoes for playing on grass. The six nylon or rubber studs are taken off—and put on—with a small wrench. The studs come in different lengths because the softer the field, or the taller the grass, the longer the studs.

Most pros inspect a grass field before a game. "I'll press a finger into the ground," says Chicago's young midfielder Rudy Glenn. "The easier it is for my finger to sink into the ground, the longer the studs I wear."

Games have been won or lost by a choice of shoes. Calgary coach Al Miller recalls a game that started on a frozen field. During the first half the sun came out and frozen turf began to thaw and turn muddy. Both teams had been wearing molded-rubber shoes but at halftime Miller's players switched to long-studded shoes. The other team came out for the second half still wearing the molded-rubber shoes. They slipped on the muddy ground while Miller's players moved with sureness, the long studs biting into the mush. One opponent tried to change direction and fell on his face, and a Calgary forward flew around him and rammed home an easy goal. Not surprisingly, Miller's team won the game.

Some stars don't like multi-studded shoes because the studs on the outside of the sole hit the hard artificial surface before the foot has kicked the ball. As a result the player loses force on kicks or passes. "What I do," says Cosmos' forward Steve Wegerle, "is have the equipment manager file off the studs on the outer rim of the sole so they don't stub the Astro-Turf."

Most soccer players insist that their shoes literally "fit like a glove." They order their soccer shoes a half-size smaller than street shoes. A few, like Chicago's Arno Steffenhagen, wear soccer shoes that are one size smaller.

But even that isn't tight enough for about half the players in the NASL. They want no "play" between their foot and the shoe when they kick a ball. After they put on their shoes before a game, they stick their feet into a basin of lukewarm water. They soak the shoes for 10 to 15 minutes. Then they walk around for half an hour. The water tightens the leather and, as it dries, it grips the foot like a second skin. After the game the shoes are soaked in oil to retain the leather's softness.

Goalkeepers are the "different" men of soccer. They can use their hands to grab the ball; the other players cannot. So the keeper will stand out in the melee around a cage and be seen by both the opposing players and the officials, they have always worn different uniforms than the other players. The traditional uniform was black, but now the keepers wear most every color in the rainbow. A Cosmos keeper like Hubert Birkenmeier, for example, has a choice of a sky blue, navy blue, or yellow shirt.

"Goalkeepers have two schools of thought about what kind of color is best," he says. "One school says you should wear a very bright color, like Day-Glo orange, for example. Some believe that if you wear a bright color, a forward will instinctively shoot the ball toward a very bright color. And so the ball will come straight into your arms. The other school of thought says that the keeper should wear as dark a color as possible. Then the forward who is kicking the ball will not see where the keeper is standing in front of the cage. If the forwad hesitates before he shoots, that is always good for the keeper. You get the chance to move to a better position and maybe someone will take the ball away from the kicker."

In Soccer Bowl 1981, the two opposing goalkeepers represented these two schools of thought. The Cosmos' Birkenmeier wore a bright yellow shirt and could be picked out easily when there was a mob around the cage. The Sting

22

keeper, Dieter Ferner, wore a powder-blue shirt that faded into the dark-green stands behind him, making him, at times, invisible. There was no clear-cut decision about which was better. Birken-meier had nine saves, Ferner eight in a game that ended after regulation and overtime play in a 0-0 tie. (In the shootout, both keepers could be seen clearly since there was nobody in front of them. The Sting won, two goals to one, and became Soccer Bowl champions.)

Until a few years ago, most goal-keepers wore gloves only during cold or rainy weather. Now they wear the gloves as routinely as first basemen wear mitts. "There are maybe a dozen companies that make different types of gloves," says Chicago's No. 2 keeper, Paul Coffee. "The ones I use are German-made. They are made of an open-cell foam substance and they are real sticky."

At a Sting practice recently I talked to Coffee about the gloves and he suggested I try them on. White, with black stripes on the back, they were five-fingered but not as tight-fitting as winter gloves. They looked and felt like the floppy gloves a car mechanic wears.

The big difference was their gummy

The Sting's goalkeeper, Paul Coffee, displays his German-made gloves.

surface. Held to my face, they felt sticky, as if they had been rubbed in bubble gum.

I picked up a ball and gripped it between the gloves. I felt I could pull away one hand and the ball would stick to the other (although, of course, it wouldn't). "Those gloves give the keeper a real sticky grip that he wouldn't have if he used only his bare hands," Coffee told me. He said most keepers wear their gloves in only one or two games, then discard them for new ones, since the stickiness wears off in handling the ball.

Until a few years ago, keepers who didn't wear gloves would often spray their hands with a sticky chemical. This was the same "stick-um" that NFL pass catchers used until it was outlawed. But now nearly all NASL keepers prefer sticky gloves to the spray. (A few spray their gloves in the belief that it makes the gloves even stickier.)

Pros rarely wear shin pads because they slow them down. But when they play on Astro-Turf, many players wrap their knees and elbows with tape. "The Astro-Turf burns when you slide on it," says Chicago forward Arno Steffenhagen. "That's why most players hate to play on it. You can't dive or slide for balls as hard as you can on grass. I don't like to

Coffee rolls on the ground after making a practice save. Even in practice most goalkeepers wear their gloves.

have my knees wrapped in tape, so what I do—and so do other players on the Sting—is splash a half a bottle of baby oil on my knees and elbows before a game. It makes your skin slicker and you can slide without getting a bad burn, what we call a 'strawberry.' "

Pros get all the soccer balls they want from their team during the season. But during the off-season many of them buy their practice balls. They suggest that you buy the best ball a company makes, because cheaper balls lose their shape quickly. The stitching between the panels is not done as well as on more expensive balls. Though balls with eight or 16 panels are available, most of the pros prefer a No. 5 ball with 32 black-and-white panels. The more panels, the easier it is for a player to see how much spin he has on the ball.

Ball in hand and fully dressed, the players are ready for the game. But there are 15 players on each NASL team, and there may be 20 or more on a high school or college team. Only 11 can play. Which 11? The coach has a list that each player with the squad wants to be on—the starting lineup.

THE LINEUP

This is the age of specialization in everything from medicine to engineering; soccer is no exception.

Soccer specialists fall into four basic groups: goalkeeper, defenders, midfielders, and forwards. Goalkeepers are rangy and sure-handed, defenders strong and nimble. Midfielders are pinpoint passers and smart playmakers, while forwards are fast and the team's hardest kickers.

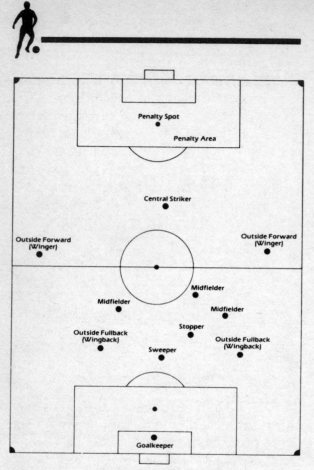

Penalty Spot

Penalty Area

Central Striker

Outside Forward
(Winger)

Outside Forward
(Winger)

Midfielder

Midfielder

Midfielder

Stopper

Outside Fullback
(Wingback)

Outside Fullback
(Wingback)

Sweeper

Goalkeeper

The approximate positions of the players on the field in a 4-3-3 formation, the most commonly used in the NASL. During a game, the players sweep up and down the field, no longer locked into a specified area. But the defenders usually position themselves on their side of the midline, the attackers on the other side.

Each player fits into a formation. The most common today is either a 4-2-4 or a 4-3-3 formation: four defenders, two or three midfielders, four or three forwards. But even within the three positions—defender, midfielder, forward—there are specialists:

DEFENDERS: The two defenders on the outside are called fullbacks or wingbacks. They mark the opposing team's outside forwards or wingers. One of the two inside forwards is called a "stopper." He marks the other team's inside forward or "striker." The striker is the other team's high scorer. So the stopper must be fast, physically tough, and be a good jumper to knock away high passes to his man. The other inside defender is the "sweeper." He plays behind the other defenders and "sweeps" up anything that gets by them—be it a ball or an attacker. The last line of the defense in front of the goalkeeper, the sweeper is a smart player who watches the action and shouts instructions to the other defenders.

MIDFIELDERS: They are often called the "brains" or the "schemers." They move the ball quickly into the

The Cosmos' winger, Seninho, brings the ball along the sideline. What all wingers must be able to do best is blast strong and accurate crossing passes to their strikers in the "sweet spot"— the penalty area in front of the goal.

other team's territory by booting passes to the forward. Like football quarterbacks, they are always looking for a way to get the ball to the free man. One midfielder is a strong attacker and two are strong defenders who can fall back to help the defense. They run longer distances than anyone else so they must have more stamina.

FORWARDS: These are the team's high scorers. The two outside forwards, "wingers," push the ball as quickly as possible toward the enemy goal. The inside forwards—strikers—lurk near the goal mouth, like pivotmen in basketball. The hardest and most accurate kicker, the striker gets a pass from the wingers and tries to ram past the keeper from six to 20 feet out.

In making out the lineup, the coach picks 11 players who can work smoothly with one another. The team is like a machine. The defenders must get the ball to the midfielders, and they must move it over to the forwards. If one unit breaks down, the machine shudders and stops.

Many of today's coaches believe that "total soccer" is just as important. They feel that soccer is not as specialized as it was 10 years ago. When Chicago Sting coach Willie Roy makes out a lineup, he may put Arno Steffenhagen at midfield. Then, halfway through the game, he may move him to sweeper. And near the end of the game he may move Steffenhagen to winger. To understand what that means, imagine Tom Seaver starting the game as a pitcher, then moving to catcher, then to the outfield—all in a nine-inning game.

"Willie Roy may have a player like Paul Hahn play two or even three positions in a game," says a member of the Sting staff. "Hahn may start as a

Forward Dave Huson circles the ball for the Sting. Coach Willie Roy will often switch him to midfield or defense during a game.

sweeper on defense, then go to winger, perhaps even to striker. You can see how this will confuse the man who is marking Hahn. He thinks Hahn will stop at midfield because Hahn started the game on defense. Instead Hahn, now a winger, charges for the other goal. For two or three seconds the confused defender leaves Hahn open. Hahn can get a pass and knock the ball into the cage. That happened to Hahn and to other Sting players three or four times in the 1981 season.

"Here is another situation created by Roy's switching. Let's suppose his starting striker is Dave Huson, who is 5-foot-9. Then, suddenly, Roy moves Huson to midfield and replaces him at striker with 6-2 Rudy Glenn. The man who was marking Huson may not be tall enough to mark Glenn, who is five inches taller than Huson. Before the other team can put a taller man on Glenn, the Sting have a height advantage around the goal. Glenn may be able to put in a header. The Sting took advantage of those mismatches in 1981 to lead the league in scoring."

In deciding his starting lineup, the coach doesn't always put down the names of his 11 best players. "Let's say I have a man who is not as good overall as another player," says Tampa Bay Rowdie coach Gordon Jago. "But he is our best at man-to-man marking. I may use him instead of the player who is a better passer and scorer. We are willing to sacrifice a goal or two if that one marker can stop an opponent who could win the game for the other side."

"You must match the right people against their people in making a lineup," says Hannes Weisweller, the coach of the Cosmos. In a playoff game against Tampa Bay in 1981, he matched defender Jeff Durgan against forward Luis Fernando and Esky Eskandarian against Frank Worthington. Fernando scored for Tampa Bay and the Cosmos lost. In the next game against Tampa Bay, the Cosmos coach switched assignments: Durgan covered Worthington, Esky marked Fernando. The Cosmos won, shutting out the Tampa Bay forwards. "Esky had the experience to handle an experienced player like Fernando," said a Cosmos player later. "Durgan didn't, being a rookie. But Durgan could mark Worthington, who is 13 years older than Durgan and slower."

The soccer coach loses much of his control over the team once the game begins. "Eighty percent of the job of the coach is finished after he has written out his lineup," says former Cosmos coach Julio Mazzei. "Plays cannot be sent in from the bench because soccer is a game of creativity. That is why it is important to have somebody out there as captain who is experienced. Once I sent in a substitute to mark Gerd Mueller. Our captain, Franz Beckenbauer, assigned the substitute to mark someone else and put another player on Mueller. Being on the field he could see that the substitute couldn't mark Mueller, but that the other player could."

Once a team starts to win with a set lineup, a coach seldom makes a change, except to replace an injured starter. "Why should I change a machine that is winning?" says former Yale University coach Hubert Vogelsinger. "If I have invented a machine that can mine gold, why should I change?"

Sting coach Willie Roy disagrees slightly. "Sometimes," he says, "I will make a change depending on whether we are playing at home or on the road. If we are on the road and I think the other side has two players who need total marking, I will put into the lineup two good defensive players. But at home you want always to attack and score, so I will use as many good offensive players as I can find." Soccer coaches, like all coaches, like to please the home-town fans—and fans like to see the home team score.

Some soccer coaches feel their job never ends. Recently Julio Mazzei was telling a friend about a phone call he got from a player when he coached the Cosmos. The player couldn't get his car started. "Imagine," says Mazzei, "he thought I was also a mechanic!"

ON THE FIELD

A super soccer player must: **1.** dribble, pass, receive the ball, and shoot; these are lumped together as ball-handling skills; **2.** know all the secrets of playing his position; and **3.** understand the strategy of team play.

Here are tips from the pros that will help you be a better player.

BALL HANDLING

One of the great dribblers of modern soccer, Johan Cruyff, played for Holland in World Cup games and for Los Angeles and Washington in the NASL. "One of my secrets," he says, "is to nudge the ball along the ground instead of kicking it when I dribble, as many players do. And you must always remember to take short, choppy steps when you run as you dribble."

Good dribblers and passers keep their heads up. "That's the trouble with too many young American players," says Franz Beckenbauer, the West German star who played for the Cosmos from 1977 to 1980. "They have their heads on their chests when they dribble and pass. You have got to be able to handle the ball without looking at it all the time. You have got to keep your head up to see what's happening around you. Look at a great player like Pelé on films and you will see that his head is always moving so that he knows where everyone on the field is."

Soccer coaches are forever yelling at their players: "Pass to feet." You must use your teammate's feet or stockings as

Paul Hahn collects a pass for the Sting. Most passes, he says, should be no more than 15 to 20 yards.

your target when you pass him the ball.

All good passers recommend using the inside of the foot to pass. "Even some good young players will try to kick the ball with the front of the foot," says George Best, the British star who played for the San Jose Earthquakes. "That's foolish. When you strike the ball with the toes, you have a smaller shoe surface than if you use the side of the foot. As a result, your passes are likely to scatter all over the place. The wider the shoe surface striking the ball, the more accurate the passes."

The instep pass calls for striking the ball with the shoelaces. It's tough to learn, but it enables a passer to bend his pass. When West Germany's Gunther Netzer sees that there is an opponent between him and a teammate, he curls the pass around the opponent. It's called a "banana pass," because of its shape. The trick is to kick the ball on its *outside* third if you are right-footed; if you kick with the left foot, kick on the ball's *inside* third. Netzer can boom a banana pass 50 yards.

Most pros recommend catching a pass on the chest. This is the easiest way to stop the ball and have it drop at your feet. The important thing in receiving a pass is to come toward the ball as it flies toward you.

"By moving to meet the pass," says Portland striker Clyde Best, one of the best in the NASL at receiving long passes, "you give yourself an extra second to collect the ball and shield it from those people trying to take it away from you. The most important thing in shielding is to position yourself between the ball and your opponent. Use whatever

The Sting's Arno Steffenhagen is on the move. "The good soccer player," he says, "always looks for someone to pass to as soon as he receives the ball."

part of the body you can, but make sure that the ball is in front of you at all times. And always keep the ball on the side of the body that is farthest from the defender. *Never* allow the ball to get between your legs where it can be kicked away by a defender."

"There is a little trick that will help you stop the ball with your chest," Pelé says. "Just before the ball hits you, fill your lungs with air and breathe out on impact, at the same time bringing your arms and shoulders forward. This coordinated movement makes your body form a sort of shell into which the ball can fall."

The great scorers of all time—Pelé, Chinaglia, Best—share one weapon: the banana kick. Like the banana pass, the banana kick curls wickedly around an opponent. In his book, *Learning Soccer with Pelé*, the great Brazilian star gave this tip on how to get off the banana kick: "Use the inside or outside of the top of the shoe for curving shots. To make the ball curve to the left with your right foot, kick it on its right side with the inside of the top of your foot; if you want to curve the ball to the left with your left foot, use the outside. If you want to make the ball curve to the right with your right foot, use the outside of the top of your shoe to kick the left side, and so on.

Ninety percent of all goals are scored within six feet of the goal. Close to the goal most shooters try to ram the ball by the keeper with as hard a kick as they can muster. Pelé offered this tip for taking a shot close to the goal: When you are close to the goal, he says, accuracy is more important than a hard shot. If you hit the ball at a hundred miles an hour and it goes straight at the keeper, his body will stop it, no matter how fast it's streaking. You can be much more accu-

On a free kick, Fort Lauderdale's Gerd Mueller gets off a banana kick to curl the ball around the wall of defenders. Note the follow-through of his kicking foot.

rate with a dinky little shot, that you can place anywhere in that living-room-sized cage you're facing.

"Using your head" in soccer means more than being smart. You can use your head to pass to a teammate or to slam the ball into the nets. "The head shot is one of the most difficult for the goalkeeper to save," says Chinaglia, the NASL's all-time leading scorer. "What I try to do, if I have time, is to place the header. Too many soccer players are concerned about getting a lot of velocity on their headers. To me, placement is more important than the speed of the shot." Like most good headers, Chinaglia heads the ball *down* toward the goalkeeper's feet.

"Practice every day to get good in the air," advises the British striker, Derek Smethurst, who played for Tampa Bay in the NASL. He suggests having a friend boot crossing passes from the left or right corners of the field. In taking crossing passes and heading the ball, he says, "jump up as high as you can; use your hips and back as well as your neck. Head toward the far post *always*—that way, if you miss it, the ball can still go in the near post. Timing is so important

B arry Wallace, the white-shirted Tulsa defender, uses his head the best way he can, getting above his opponent with his arms wide and heading the ball with the top of his skull. Most of the time, however, the ball should be headed with the top of the forehead, eyes open.

45

too: if you can get up a fraction of a second before your opponent, you've beaten him. The *force* of your body pushes him down. Try to hang up there—learn how to go up and hang. Always watch the other player to see when he's going up—try to be on his blind side so he can't see you—and then go up an instant before he does. This will improve your air play immensely, just this simple emphasis on getting up in the air a fraction of a second before your defender.''

Most high scorers recommend aiming goal shots at the corners of the cage and keeping the kick low. "Low shots are the most difficult for the keeper to stop,'' says Karl-Heinz Granitza of the Sting. "He has to go down, as well as left or right for the ball, and that may take a split-second too much time. Also, when you boot a ball along the ground, it can take a bounce that's lucky for you."

Granitza recommends pointing the toe down to keep the ball low. And, as with the pass, most good shots are kicked with the inside of the foot. "But everything's a weapon when you're trying to score,'' Smethurst once said. "I've knocked in goals with my shins, my knees, even my backside."

PLAYING YOUR POSITION

Goalkeeper

"Those soccer oddities," soccer journalist Paul Gardner once wrote of keepers, "those players who use their hands in a game where everyone else uses their feet."

Their job: to stop a ball going as fast as 60 miles an hour from entering an area that is as big as a living room. The soccer cage is eight feet high and 24 feet wide, a space of 192 yawning square feet.

"The key to being a good goalkeeper," says Gene DuChateau, an American-born keeper who played for Tulsa and other NASL teams, "is talking to your defenders. The keeper is the last line of defense. He can see it all, so he is the one who must tell the defenders where to go. And the defenders must follow his orders. The keeper is the only one who can spot an opponent who is open. He can tell the defender that danger is right behind him or that he has the time to clear the ball or to pass it to someone else. The keeper can even tell a defender where the ball should be passed

Fort Lauder-
dale keeper
Jan Van Beveren
watches the ac-
tion come close.
"You've got to be
the boss in the
penalty area," he
says. "The extra
thing is to read
the game...."

next. The good goalkeeper has got to
direct his defense with confidence and
with the authority of a boss."

"You've got to be the boss in the
penalty area," agrees Jan Van Beveren of
the Fort Lauderdale Strikers. The penalty area is the keeper's domain, that
rectangle of ground that's 44 yards wide
and 18 yards deep in front of the cage.
"The average goalkeeper can stop shots.
The extra thing is to read the game, to
know what's going on, to know all the

players and what they can do, your own players and the opponents.''

Sting goalkeeper Dieter Ferner lunges for a low shot toward the corner, probably the most difficult for a goalkeeper to stop.

''Scream when there's action around your goal mouth,'' says Hubert Birkenmeier of the Cosmos. ''I yell so much that after some games my throat is sore and my voice is hoarse. The defenders need advice, so they ask me to shout at them. Sure, I get mad when they don't do what I want, but you've got to learn to trust one another, to play together.''

One of the biggest perils for a keeper is allowing the mind to wander when the action is fast and furious at the other end of the field. ''When there's nothing to do,'' says Volkmar Gross, who has tended goal for the San Diego Sockers, ''that's when to concentrate most of all. When the ball is down at the other end of the field for a long time, I follow it closely, playing the game in my mind.'' To keep himself alert Gross takes a walk around the penalty area. The Cosmos' Birkenmeier jogs around the boundary lines of the penalty area. ''Then I talk to myself,'' he once told Paul Gardner. ''Otherwise I might find myself looking up into the stands, and that's no good.''

''There is no question that the hardest part of goalkeeping is to keep your mind from wandering when things are quiet in your half,'' former NASL keeper Alan Mayer says. He offers this tip for fixing the mind on the game: ''Try to play a little game with yourself in which you're a soccer analyst describing on the radio what's happening down at the other end of the field. That way your mind is always on the game. If you get caught daydreaming, you're going to let a goal through."

From the physical point of view, the toughest plays for a keeper are: **1.** crossing passes from the corner that fly across the goal mouth; and **2.** the one-on-one match against a shooter. Birkenmeier of-

Tampa Bay keeper Winston DuBose shows off his white rubber gloves and the elasticity of his legs as he leans a long way to his left to stop a shot. One trick of keepers is to feint one way, showing the shooter a lot of net on the other side, then come back to cover up what they have teasingly shown.

51

fers this tip on handling crossing passes:

"Wait a second or two before you make the decision to go out to catch the pass or to stay in the goal mouth. That way you can see just how far you have to go and whether you can get the ball. Also you should leap off one foot, not two, the way the good high-jumpers do. This gives you maximum height. And you can use the other leg as a defense to keep people away who might try to knock you down."

The goalkeeper's nightmare: penalty kicks. Here Fort Lauderdale's Ray Hudson rams by the ball by Portland's Jim Gorsek.

Going one-on-one against a shooter only 12 feet away, the keeper is obviously going to lose the penalty kick at least as often as he wins. Some keepers try to psych out the kicker. "Walk to the side of the goal," suggests Tampa Bay coach Gordon Jago. "Refuse to be ready when the kicker is ready, make noises—in short, provide any kind of distractions that will unsettle the kicker who is already under pressure, all eyes on him."

During a penalty kick the keeper is tied down by another rule: He cannot move before the ball is kicked. "The secret," says one keeper, "is that even though we are not supposed to move our feet, you have to move just before the kick is taken or you are a dead duck. The officials let us get away with it as long as the move isn't too obvious. And we can legally move our bodies, swaying left or right to induce the kicker to shoot to one side. Then we react and go to that side."

The shootout is another one-on-one situation for the keeper. A shootout occurs when a game is tied after regulation play and overtime. Five shooters on each side try for goals. The side that puts the most balls into the cage wins the game. In a shootout, the keeper can move be-

Cosmos goalkeeper Hubert Birkenmeier shows how to kick a ball out of the penalty area to a teammate. The ball can be kicked farther than it can be thrown, but long kicks often are intercepted.

fore the shot.

"Come out quickly, but don't commit yourself," advises the Sting's Paul Coffee. "Wait for the kicker's move." Says San Diego's Volkmar Gross: "I race out as fast as I can to the penalty spot (12 feet from the cage). Then I move forward more slowly, trying to make myself look bigger than I am, spreading my arms out, so that it looks like there's nothing left to shoot at except me. I like to try to get them to dribble around me. I can often tackle them and knock the ball away with a sliding tackle. A shot is much more difficult to block."

"As you go out at the kicker in the shootout," suggests Hubert Birkenmeier, "remind yourself not to go down until you are sure he has kicked the ball. If you go down and the shooter still has the ball, it's a sure goal. He can kick the ball over you or dribble around you and kick the ball into the empty cage. In a shootout, you must have a lot of confidence."

"Confidence," NASL keeper Alan Mayer, once said, "is 85 percent of goalkeeping." That confidence is never more important than in the one-on-one situation in which the shooter has broken through the last line of defense and races toward the cage. "If the shooter is coming in from the right side," another American-born keeper, Tony Chursky, says, "the smart goalkeeper comes out moving to his right side. He forces the shooter to go for the far corner. And you try to get him to go to his 'weak' foot. You sometimes can do that by playing him at such an angle, or by coming out so far, that he has to switch the ball to his other foot, the 'weak' foot, in order to have a

Cosmos goalkeeper Hubert Birkenmeier watches the action, his intensity showing in his face.

better angle to shoot.''

Another former NASL goalkeeper, the Bronx-born Shep Messing, had unique ideas about goalkeeping. He once gave this tip to keepers: ''When a shot is a sure goal, dive anyway. It will make you look good to your coach.''

He was just as original in his advice to keepers facing a Chinaglia or George Best one-on-one: ''Rush out in a half-crouch toward the attacker, screaming at him. This not only narrows the angle, but makes him hurry."

Other tips from Messing:

1. Establish your authority in the area right away. This means shouting instructions loudly and decisively to your defenders and getting a piece of any opponent who wants to rub shoulders with you.

2. Don't nonchalant any shots. Even the simplest ground ball can take an unexpected bounce and make you look like a fool. Always get down on one knee so your body and your hands are behind the ball.

3. When jumping for a high ball, extend both arms in the direction of the ball and try to catch it at the top of your leap.

4. On diving saves, try to dive out at a 45-degree angle rather than flat across the goal mouth. Make sure your forearm and the ball touch the ground first. Always protect yourself by ending up with the ball cradled to your chest rather than outstretched where an opponent can kick it.

5. When diving for a shot below your waist, lead with your left hand. If the shot is above the waist, throw the opposite hand over to give your body momentum.

6. When coming out for a crossing pass, if you are not one hundred percent sure you can catch the ball, punch it as far away as possible, or tip it over the crossbar with your fingertips.

7. After catching a ball, try to get rid of it as quickly as possible by throwing it on a low line drive to an unmarked teammate who can start a quick counter attack.

8. Never relax. Even when the action is at the other end of the field, your concentration must be intense. A good goalkeeper doesn't smile for 90 minutes.

But perhaps the shrewdest bit of advice comes from Great Britain's Phil Parkes, who once told Paul Gardner and David Hirshey in *Sport* magazine: "I always try to make a save look easy. If you can make it look easy, that just makes your opponent sick. If he thinks he's hit a great shot and you just casually pick it off, he's bound to think 'What do I have to do to beat this guy?' "

Defender

Next to the goalkeeper, the four defenders—the two wingbacks, the stopper, and the sweeper—are usually the biggest men on the team. Playing near the sidelines for much of the game, the two wingbacks must be the fastest defenders as they try to glue themselves to the attacking wingers, or outside forwards, as they are also called. The stopper roams the middle, and he must be a good header, to butt away high shots, as well as an all-around tough player to mark the other team's heavy hitter—the striker. Behind the defense—and just in front of the keeper—is the sweeper, who calls out instructions to the other three and looks to tackle any ball or body that gets by them.

At least that's the way it looks on paper. In today's game of "total soccer," however, "it is no longer enough for a defender to be a rock-like figure in the middle," England's great Jack Charlton has said. "He must be able to pick out the point of danger in his own penalty area and have the quick pounce with which to kill it."

And their half of the field is no longer a prison for the four defenders. Now any of the four defenders, especially the sweeper, can charge across the midfield line and be part of the attack.

This sudden switch in roles—the defender turning quickly into an attacker—was best illustrated by Franz Beckenbauer when he played for West Germany in the early 1970s. He got the idea while watching defender Giacinto Facchetti play for Inter Milan of Italy in 1962. "At that time there was no sweeper," he recalls. "Everyone played man-to-man, everyone stuck to his position. Facchetti made many runs from left fullback on defense into attack. But it was only him and I thought, 'Why not the right fullback? This is beautiful soccer, a defender playing like an attacker.' So in 1964 I started to attack from sweeper."

Tampa Bay defender Mike Connell is one of the best in the league at charging from the defense to the offense—what the pros call "overlapping." "It will happen maybe two or three times in a game," says Connell. "You get the ball, look upfield, and see nothing but empty space in front of you. There's no one who can tackle you, then take the ball away from you and go around you to attack the keeper one-on-one. That's when you make the overlapping run. You can't plan for overlapping runs before a game. But if a defender sees a chance to attack and score, he should take the chance.''

But Connell, Beckenbauer, and other defenders add these warnings on overlapping:

1. You must know what you are doing.

Tampa Bay's Mike Connell takes off on one of his "overlapping" forays. He says that "if a defender sees a chance to attack and score, he should take the chance."

2. One of your teammates—a midfielder or even an attacker—must fall back to fill your hole in the defensive wall.

3. Whenever possible, finish an overlapping run with a shot on goal; that will give you the time to get back to your defensive area.

4. In any case, get back as fast as possible.

But, as exciting and as profitable as overlapping runs can be to a team, a defender's first job is to defend. "What you never want to happen," says Werner Roth, a former Cosmos defender and now a film actor *(Victory!)*, "is let your man get around you. What helps is to have a strong sweeper behind you. I had a great sweeper behind me, Carlos Alberto, when I was with the Cosmos. I always knew if I lost my man for a moment, he would be there to cover for me."

Knowing how to tackle—booting the ball away from an opponent—is especially important for a defender. "Lots of players don't realize this, but tackling is one of the few times in soccer when you should kick the ball with your toes," says Sting defender Paul Hahn. "As you slide toward the ball, if you kick it with the front part of your foot, you are getting an extra inch or two of reach with your leg."

When do you tackle? If you leave your feet to slide and tackle an opponent, he can go right around you if you miss the ball. Most pros agree that the best time to tackle is when the ball-handler has to stop or when the ball has bounded

Defender Keith Weller (14) of the Strikers shows how close the good defender marks his man. Tampa Bay midfielder Wes McLeod has turned for the ball and Weller is moving with him in almost perfect synchronization. Note Weller's long-studded shoes.

Cosmos defender Jeff Durgan keeps the ball close to him after making a tackle and recovering the ball. Too many defenders, even among the pros, get rid of the ball too quickly by booting a long pass, says former Cosmos defender Werner Roth.

a considerable distance ahead of the dribbler. "Those are the times," says Werner Roth, "when the forward has the least chance to beat you by going around you."

Too many defenders attempt to boot the ball as far away from an opponent as possible—and as quickly as possible. In most cases, says Roth, that only hands the ball back to your opponent. A hasty kick is usually not aimed properly and a long kick across the midline is most likely to land at the feet of the other team's midfielders.

"The tendency of most inexperienced defenders is to kick the ball as quickly as possible when they get it," Roth once said. "I know I used to want to just get rid of it when I got the ball, and many times my pass was inaccurate and wasted. Franz Beckenbauer showed me that I had a couple of seconds to spare most of the time and that this is the time to look and find somebody open."

Most defenders try to pass no more than 15 to 20 yards. "After that," says Paul Hahn, "you don't have the accuracy you want, for one thing, and of course the longer the pass, the easier it is to intercept it."

But one defender who occasionally let loose with a long boomer deep into the territory of the other team was Santiago Formosa, who played for New York, Los Angeles, and Houston. "I only did it on artificial surfaces," he says. "On the rug you get a good bounce and a long roll. And I only did it when I saw that one of my forwards was open at the other end of the field. I tried to get the ball in front of him so that he would have a breakaway run at the keeper."

But Formosa kept most of his passes short. "Your first thought should be to

Tulsa defender Victor Moreland (18) throws a legal shoulder charge at the Minnesota Kicks' Ruben Pagnanini. Be careful, say defenders, in charging. Hitting with the elbows or the hands is illegal.

pass straight ahead," he says, "to your midfielder or forward. If that can't be done, you should pass to the right or left. If all the midfielders are covered, then you pass to another defender in the middle of the field—the stopper or the sweeper. Or you pass back to the goalkeeper if nobody else is open. But be careful with your passes in front of your own goal. Those passes should *always* be short."

Most young defenders have the same question when they talk to the pros: "How close should I mark?" Bob Smith, who played for Philadelphia and New York, suggests: "Mark your man right out of the game. Mark him so tightly that he *never* gets the ball. If he never gets the ball, then you will never have to stop a shot by him on goal."

In one game several years ago, Smith marked his man so closely "he was inside his shorts half the time," one observer later said. There was a halt in play, and Smith's man walked to a water fountain to gulp some water. When he finished drinking he looked up, and there—right beside him—stood Smith.

As a rule of thumb, most coaches suggest a defender keep a yard between

himself and the man with the ball. "A good rule for defenders," says Gordon Jago, coach of the Tampa Bay Rowdies, "is that the farther their man is from the ball, the looser they mark him. The

Striker defender Ken Fogarty wins the ball. In their battles with strikers, defenders try to stay on the side of the kicker's strong foot so that if he or she gets a pass, the ball will be on the weak foot.

looser they mark him when he doesn't have the ball, the more coverage they can give to other areas of the field.''

In marking, the worst mistake a defender can make, says Jago, ''is becoming a ball chaser.'' He cites this example: A ball bounces across the penalty area and a defender chases after the ball. ''Leaving a man unmarked in that area,'' says Jago, ''is asking for a goal.''

Some other tips from defenders:

1. Try to force a winger to the sideline. Keep the winger from coming inside—the ''sweet spot'' for scorers.

2. If possible, keep a striker from facing your goal. Crowd the striker so he can't turn.

3. Try to position yourself between the wing and striker, cutting off the wing's passing route.

4. Tackle with both legs when you can.

''It's also important,'' sums up Roth, ''for the whole defense to work as a unit and for the midfielders to come back to support the defender. If I know I have help to the rght or to the left, or that there is somebody behind me ready to cover, I can move in closer to the forward and crowd him. When we crowd him we can force him to use the left foot if he is a right footer."

Midfielder

While defenders and forwards run about five miles, a middle fielder runs over six miles during a game. "The defenders stay on their side of the midfield line most of the time," says Tampa Bay midfielder Wes McLeod. "The forwards stay mostly in the other team's territory. Neither the defenders nor the forwards cross the midfield line very often. We're crossing it all game long, rushing into the other team's side to help the forwards on attack, then falling back into our territory to help the defense when we're being attacked. It's not unusual for a midfielder to run the entire length of the field, more than a hundred yards, *twice* in a few minutes of action."

Fitness is the first rule for midfielders. Determination is the second. "The big thing is determination," says McLeod. "There's a pain barrier. It hits you usually in the second half. Some guys can't go through it. It's tough. But I want to attack and defend, to run the full 90 minutes, so I keep really fit."

In the ideal midfield, Franz Beckenbauer once said, "you need one playmaker and two or three players who will run, who will make it difficult for the opposing team." By running, the other midfielders take opponents with them

The tackle that failed. Two opponents tried to tackle the Cosmos' Franz Beckenbauer and steal the ball, but he flies over them. They are momentarily out of action, and the ball is within range of the swooping Franz.

and open up spaces. The playmaker shoots the ball into those areas. "A good midfielder," says the Cosmos' midfielder Vladislav Bogicevic, "tries to create what we call a 'team advantage.' You force a defender to choose which of two

Cosmos midfielder Vladislav Bogicevic runs for the ball. Playing the most exhausting position in soccer, Bogey tries to save a portion of his energy for the end of the game. "Most games," he says, "are won or lost in the last 10 minutes."

strikers to cover. Then you get the ball to the striker who is open."

"You have got to have good vision,"

says Tampa Bay's McLeod. "You need to know where people are to give them the ball." Says Bogicevic: "It is very important for a midfielder to have what we call a 'fast ball.' This means that his passes are very hard and fast, and so they are difficult to intercept." Adds British star Allan Clarke: "Great midfield players can pinpoint a pass to anywhere on the pitch."

"Keep these two things in mind if you are a midfielder," Beckenbauer once said. "When the other team has the ball, stay with your man. Mark him. When your team has the ball, you must anticipate where your teammates will go. You must know the players."

"You play about half the time on defense and half the time on offense," says Bogey Bogicevic. "But your primary task is to defend."

Not all midfielders agree that defense is their most important job. Says Rodney Marsh, the British midfielder who played for Tampa Bay: "A good midfield player may lack defensive discipline if he is playing with two midfielders who have good defensive ability. The middle midfielder is usually the architect. He yells instructions to the other players on attack. He assists on goals and he also scores goals, but as much as possible he creates the chances for the forwards to score goals."

Beckenbauer and other players suggest these two drills for midfielders:

Cosmos midfielder Rick Davis shows his slide-tackling form. By making contact with the ball, Davis forces his opponent, the Kicks' Tim Twellman, to avoid his legs. If Twellman trips over Davis's leg before Davis contacts the ball, a foul will be called against Davis.

1. Five players line up against another five players. A sixth player joins one of the squads. He is the midfielder for this drill. He passes the ball to the other players on his squad. When they receive the ball, they pass it back to him, since he is unmarked. The drill teaches the midfielder how to control the game, how he can slow it down or speed it up.

2. The one-touch drill has two five-player squads line up against each other with no goals. Each player must pass to a teammate after only one touch of the ball. The players learn how to pass as long as 40 yards and, most important, how to anticipate a teammate's position.

"The worst thing that can happen to a midfielder," says Steve Ralbovsky, who played for Chicago and Colorado in the NASL, "is to get caught out of position. Midfielders should play simple and safe, a plain game aimed at keeping possession of the ball above all."

Other tips to midfielders from NASL players and coaches:

1. Try to cross the ball to the opposite side of the field when there is congestion around the ball on your side.

2. On defense you usually have at least one defender behind you. Be aware of where he is at all times. If he is in proper position, be bold and try to swipe the ball from a forward with a tackle. If he is out of position, be more conservative. Try to slow down the forward. And if the forward gets by you, don't stand there. Fall back to mark someone else so the defense won't be overwhelmed.

3. When you have the ball, look first for the open winger on either side of the pitch.

4. If no one is open, try passing to an inside forward, drawing the defense toward the inside. Call for a return pass and get the ball to the outside before the defenders can react. As the defense moves toward the sidelines, areas will open up in the penalty area—the "sweet spot," where strikers work the ball for shots on goal.

5. Don't be reluctant to backheel the ball to a defender if your forwards are covered. Then move upfield, opening space between yourself and your defender so you can receive the return pass and move the ball into the opponent's territory.

6. When one of your defenders "overlaps"—speeds toward the opposing goal—it's the midfielder's responsibility to fall back and fill the hole. You should always know where your four fullbacks are.

7. Drive the defensive play to the outside as much as you can. If you can keep the opposing player on the outside, it limits the space the attacker can work, because his back is to the sideline.

Midfielders are the thinkers as well as the legs of a soccer team. "If you don't use your head," says the Cosmos' Vladislav Bogicevic, "your feet won't be of any use to you on the soccer field."

Forward

Most teams use three or four forwards: two wingers on the outside and one or two strikers on the inside.

Strikers do most of the scoring. On the attack, says NASL all-time high scorer Giorgio Chinaglia, "you are a scoring animal. You must think of only one thing: scoring. Keep the ball low, because low shots are the toughest for goalkeepers to stop. There's luck involved in scoring, but there's also an old saying in soccer: You make your own luck. Look for the loose ball and when you get it, kick it as soon as you can and as hard as you can.

"Don't aim. You don't have time to think of things like that. If I do aim, I aim only a yard on either side of the keeper. If the shot is hard, he has no chance."

Chinaglia lashes a shot at the goal. Note the twist of his kicking foot, the ball having been kicked at the shoe laces. A good striker, he says, "has to be a scoring animal."

But with defenders swarming all around the striker, there is little room to get off a hard shot. "The closer you move toward the opponent's goal, the harder it is to play, that's a fact," says former British star Rodney Marsh, a high scorer for Tampa Bay. "When you get to the last third of the field, they'll kick you, punch you, do anything to keep you from scoring."

In the middle of those melees, the striker must keep his cool and focus his sights on the goal. "Some guys rush things and make a mess of it," says South African striker, Derek Smethurst, who has played in the NASL. "But you've got a fraction of a second more than you think. You would be surprised how many defenders freeze in the box, just stand there and do nothing."

All strikers agree: To be a high scorer, you must have confidence. "You have to really believe that you can score in every minute of the game," says Steve David, who led the league in scoring in 1975. "If you don't score with two chances, you've got to be even more confident about the third chance." "And remember," adds Giorgio Chinaglia, "for every one time you are a hero, you are a bum five times."

There are many ways a player can score. As Derek Smethurst says, you can even put a ball into the cage with your backside. But most goals are scored with the head or the feet.

Forward Oscar Fabbiani, playing here for Tampa Bay, dribbles by a defender. The trick, say the good dribblers, is to nudge the ball rather than kick it.

One of the NASL's best headers, Paul Child, has played for Atlanta and Mem-

The Cosmos' Wilhelmus Rijsbergen shows the instep kick, the kick used most often by the pros. The ball is struck at the shoelaces. Note that the toes must be pointed slightly outward or the foot will stub the ground.

phis. "I have a secret," he once said. "When I see that the man with the ball is going to put up a high crossing pass in front of the goal mouth, I make a run toward the goalpost at a 45-degree angle.

That way I can see both the goal and my teammate with the ball."

He always tries to head the ball toward the goalkeeper's feet. "Get above the ball," he says. "Strike it with your forehead about an inch above the eyebrows. Make sure you keep your eyes

Tulsa's Duncan McKenzie, a midfielder and forward, keeps the ball close to him as he dribbles. "The closer you are marked," he says, "the closer you must keep the ball to you."

open. Too many players, even pros, shut their eyes. You can't aim if you can't see. Nod it downward. It's much more difficult for a keeper to handle a ball at his feet."

"On a header," says Bob Smith, another NASL veteran, "go up with your elbows out so that your opponent can't get too close to you. And *always* think to yourself: I am going to win the ball."

The bicycle kick is the most spectacular kick in soccer. No one could bicycle kick better than Pelé. Because the kicker gets off this shot with his *back* to the goal, it usually surprises the keeper, and the ball flies by before the keeper has even seen it.

Pelé describes the bicycle kick: "It should only be attempted on soft ground and you should practice it in sand or some other very soft surface. With your back to the cage, fling your legs forward and upward as the ball floats down toward you. One leg should be higher. The lower leg then comes up to kick the ball over your head toward the goal. Now you are coming down with your back parallel to the grass. You hit with your fingers spread out to cushion the fall, then land on your forearms and finally your back."

The bicycle kick, the pros warn, should be attempted only by experienced players. "But once you've scored on a bicycle kick," says Derek Smethurst, "it will be a goal you'll never forget."

The striker almost always takes the penalty kick. Pelé was one of the greatest penalty kickers. "There are only 12 yards between the penalty spot and the goal," he wrote in his book, *Learning Soccer with Pelé*. "And you can't be marked, so the advantage is all yours. The goal is eight yards wide. The goalkeeper, in the middle, can cover only about three to four of those yards. That leaves a gap of two yards on his left or on his right that he can't cover. Put the ball into the left gap or right gap of the cage and you have a sure goal."

When a game is tied after regulation play, the NASL and some amateur teams have a shootout. Five players from each side get one kick at the goal. The team that scores the most goals wins the game. The players charge at the keeper from the 35-yard line and must kick within five seconds. The goalkeeper is allowed to run out toward the kicker, trying to smother the ball before it's kicked or forcing the kicker to take a shot wide of the mark.

One of the NASL's best shootout

scorers is Minnesota's Stewart Jump, who scored on four of five shootout attempts during one season. "The secret is in the first touch of the ball," he says. "You push the ball far enough ahead of you so that you can make the big move on your second touch of the ball. But don't push the ball too far ahead, or the goalkeeper will get to the ball first. On that second touch you are either going to kick it or fake a kick to get the keeper to dive to the ground. If he's down, you can dribble around him for an easy goal at the empty cage or kick it over him."

TEAM WORK

A soccer victory usually goes to the team that runs the hardest and the longest. "Soccer is like chess played at 90 miles an hour," Pelé once said. "But the pieces are human beings. The pieces have to make their own moves and they can't spend 10 minutes thinking about what to do."

In a 90-minute game, says Chinaglia, "you're lucky if you get the ball for three minutes. You have to know what to do during the other 87 minutes."

"When you are waiting for the play

to come your way, you should *never* be standing still," Derek Smethurst said during an interview with writer Lowell

The perfect pass for a striker comes at him on the fly while he runs straight at the goalkeeper. This pass to Giorgio Chinaglia is on the fly and he can volley it with tremendous force toward the cage. And the defender is beside, not in front of him.

Miller. "I try to get myself in good position—get into the open space—before the play gets close to me. I make my move as inconspicuous as possible—I actually try to hide what I am doing when I move around. This means I don't call for the ball too much because this telegraphs the play....

"The best place to be with a defender—and I always try to maneuver myself there—is one or two yards behind him (keeping offside problems in mind). You must remember that the defender can only react *to* you, not *before* you, so that when you make your move you are going to get a three-yard jump on him.... If he tries to come back around and get behind you (this is where any good defender should be), then you can just walk around behind him again. Go in circles behind him all the way to the goal line if you have to, but get behind that man."

The players maneuver constantly to get free, but unlike football, soccer has few set plays. When you do get free, you must now depend on a teammate to get the ball to you. "That," says Chinaglia, "is what teamwork is all about."

"Teamwork in soccer," Franz Beckenbauer once said, "comes down to a very simple thing: getting two of your men in a situation where there is only one of their men."

That requires quick, sudden movement of the ball from one area of the field to another that is empty or lightly

The Cosmos' Seninho takes off on an attack—without the ball. "For 97 percent of the game," says his teammate, Giorgio Chinaglia, "you don't have the ball. What will you be doing durng that time—signing autographs? You must know how to move without the ball to get free for a pass."

guarded. The long 50-yard pass can sometimes result in two attackers facing one fullback. But there is always the danger of being offside with a long pass. (A player is offside if there are fewer than two opponents between him and the goal he is attacking when he receives a pass.)

That's why the pros prefer the short "wall" pass, or the "give and go." "No man can run as fast as a ball can be passed," says Derek Smethurst, "and defenders have no time to react to a quick, perfectly executed wall pass.... Give and go, give and go—if the ball bounces right, you're all alone for a shot."

The wall pass comes from the British drill of kicking the ball against a wall at an angle, then running to receive the ball as it rebounds from the wall at another angle. In a game, the "wall" is another teammate. You pass the ball to him, then go by your defender with a quick burst of speed and receive the return pass.

"The good soccer player," says the Sting's Arno Steffenhagen, "always looks for someone to pass the ball to as soon as he receives a pass. You are not going to go around as many defenders with a dribble as you are with a wall pass. Two players, getting off perfect wall passes, can go by 10 men."

Once, during a game in Brazil, Pelé weaved through an entire team *all by himself* to score a goal. When he had to pass, he bounced the ball off the shins of

Tulsa's Barry Wallace (3) juts out a foot to trap a pass. The quick "give-and-go" pass, say the pros, is the best way to move the ball into areas where there are two of your players and only one of theirs.

opponents, took the rebound and swept goalward. But not even Pelé scored on solo runs very often. In fact, there is a plaque inside the stadium commemorating that goal. Even for Pelé, soccer was always a team game.

POST-GAME
WRAP-UP

Frantz Mathieu stared at the TV screen, an intense look on his lean, bony face. He was watching a videotape replay of a Chicago Sting-New York Cosmos game played a few weeks earlier in the 1981 season. A defender for the Sting, Frantz fixed his eyes on the high-scoring Cosmos player, Giorgio Chinaglia. He watched how Chinaglia hung near the goal mouth and looked for high crossing passes that he could head into the cage. Frantz noted that Chinaglia seldom crossed the midfield line to help the defense. Frantz decided that the next time he marked Chinaglia, he would stick close to him even when the Sting had the ball in Cosmos territory. "Otherwise," he told a teammate, "a Cosmos can boom a long pass to him if they get back the ball and see him unmarked."

"By watching the replay," Frantz said later, "and by thinking about what he'd done in other games I'd played against him, I knew what I must do for the Soccer Bowl.

In Soccer Bowl 1981—the Sting versus the Cosmos for the NASL championship—Sting coach Willie Roy told Frantz to "totally mark" Chinaglia. That meant shadowing Chinaglia closely, hanging at his elbow, keeping the ball away from him. Frantz marked Chinaglia so totally that the league's all-time top scorer could get off only one shot and didn't score a single goal as the Sting triumphed, 1-0.

"I thought a lot about how I had played him in the other games," Frantz said after the victory. "In those other games I had played maybe 60 percent defense and 40 percent offense. I decided I had to play more defense against him. In the Soccer Bowl I played maybe 15 percent offense and 85 percent defense."

Post-game analysis—deciding which strategies worked and which didn't—is a big part of today's soccer.

Defender Frantz Mathieu gets off an outside-of-the-foot pass.

Like football, baseball, and basketball coaches, soccer coaches study game films to see what their team did right and where it went wrong. Individual players look at films to see how they got the ball by the keeper or how the keeper made the save. Keepers study replays to see how they were scored on.

In that regular-season Sting-Cosmos game, the teams were tied after regulation play. Sting forward Rudy Glenn faked going to his left, dribbled to his right, then shot the ball with his right foot past Cosmos goalkeeper Hubert Birkenmeier's left shoulder.

Later, both Birkenmeier and Glenn watched videotapes and replayed that shot in their minds as they prepared for the rematch in the Soccer Bowl. "I made up my mind that if there was another shootout," says Glenn, "I would again kick the ball with my right foot. That's the only one I like to use in shootouts. But I dediced that I would fake going to the right side."

The two did face each other in a Soccer Bowl shootout. Standing in front of the cage, Birkenmeier watched carefully as Glenn put down the ball on the 35-yard line. Birkenmeier reminded himself, "he likes to go to my left."

Looking down at the ball, Glenn told himself not to change his plan to shoot at the right side. "You make your plan," he said later, "and you follow it."

The official dropped his flag. Push-

Rudy Glenn brings the ball across the midfield area for the Sting. "You make your plan," he says, "and you follow it."

ing the ball in front of him, Glenn charged toward the goalkeeper as Birkenmeier ran out to meet him. Glenn faked to the right, swung left, and kicked. The ball swerved by Birkenmeier's flopping right glove and crashed into the nets. That shootout goal won the championship for the Sting.

"I firmly believe in studying films of games to improve the peformances of players," says veteran coach Hubert Vogelsinger. "What I like to do is scissor out what a player does wrong. I only show the player what he did right. If a keeper does a good job on handling a high crossing pass and then he does a bad job on another cross, I would only show him the tape of his good performance. Mistakes are always going to be made, but I want the film to show him how he does something right, not how he does something wrong. He isn't going to learn how to do it right by watching himself do it wrong. He will only learn by watching how he does it right."

"Soccer players don't watch replays of games as often as football players do," says Charlie Fajkus, another Sting midfielder. "And I think that's a mistake. I would love to have a video cassette to watch what I do right and what I do wrong, see the strengths and weaknesses of other players. We play some teams and I don't know a thing about them."

KEEPING
IN SHAPE

"The one ingredient in soccer that hasn't changed from the time when you would run from one village to the other is *stamina*. And it is the main ingredient in soccer—more so than size or speed. In soccer you have to prepare yourself for physical exhaustion. I probably lose 11 or 12 pounds a game and run seven or eight miles. I've never played in a sport that demands a player to be in better physical condition.

—*Kyle Rote Jr., when he played for the Dallas Tornado*

"Soccer is often a footrace to the ball."
—*Innumerable soccer coaches*

Between games—and even between seasons—soccer players must train vigo-
rously to keep their bodies in top
condition for what is probably the most
exhausting of all American team sports.
Most do what the Cosmos' Steve Wegerle
does when the season ends. "I stay away
from soccer," he says. "I go back to
South Africa and I play tennis, golf,
swim. I don't even look at a soccer ball for
two or three weeks. Then, when it's time
to rejoin the Cosmos, I begin to do a lot of
running, as much as five miles or more a
day. And I will go to the soccer field and
begin to work on my passing and shoot-
ing. Up until then, the last thing I want to
see is a soccer ball."

During the season, however, a soccer ball is never far from a player's foot.
"Kicking the ball," says Sting coach Willie Roy, "that's where the fun is, that's
where the magic of soccer is. We all like
to kick the ball and see where it will go.
That's a joy."

To make the hard work of keeping in
shape fun for the players, most NASL

and amateur coaches recommend conditioning drills in which the players kick the ball.

The New York Cosmos like to play a game that Giorgio Chinaglia calls Bull in the Middle (sometimes called Pig in the Middle). Four or five players stand inside a large square, 10 yards on each side. The corners of the square are marked with flags or uniform shirts. Inside the square stand two players—the "bulls."

The Cosmos play Bull in the Middle during practice. The shirts on the ground mark the boundaries of the square. Giorgio Chinaglia, at left, controls the ball as one of the bulls (middle) sprints toward him.

The four or five players kick the ball among them. They must keep the ball inside the square. The two bulls try to intercept the ball, or force a kicker to kick the ball outside the square. When that happens—a ball is intercepted or it flies out of bounds—the player who kicked the ball becomes one of the bulls in the middle and one of the bulls joins the players on the outside.

"The bulls have to do a lot of stop-and-start running to intercept the ball," says Chinaglia, "so the drill is good for their legs and stamina. The guys on the outside get to practice their short passes. And the two bulls have to team together to trap somebody and steal the ball, which is good for their defense."

Other pros like the drill "shadow play." "It's similar to what the boxers do when they shadow box," says Paul Coffee of the Sting. "You match yourself against your shadow, which is 'marking' you. You dribble down the field with the ball. You twist, turn, stop, start, turn left, turn right, turn every which way, trying to get away from your shadow. You can't, of course, but shadow play is great for sharpening your agility, your speed off the ball, and your endurance."

Most soccer pros have exercises they do by themselves or with a teammate. Here are six designed to improve agility:

1. Squeeze the ball between your ankles. Jump, and as you jump, toss the ball from your ankles into your hands. Bend and place the ball on the ground. Repeat the drill and each day increase the number of times you can flip the ball upward without a muff.

2. Squeeze the ball between your ankles. Jump, arching your back so that you flip the ball backwards, over your back and catch the ball as it bounces in front of you. Try to do that at least five straight times without a miss. If you are working with a teammate, you can pass the ball to him.

3. Toss the ball up into the air and collect it on your chest. Let it roll down your body to your feet, then take off on a quick 10-yard dribble. Repeat an increasing number of times.

4. Stretch out on the ground, one leg bent. With that leg, kick the ball into the air. Jump up and catch the ball over your head. Repeat as often as possible.

5. One player stands holding the ball. The other is stretched out on the ground, both legs high in the air. The first player tosses the ball. The player on the ground does a backward roll, leaps into the air and heads the ball back to the first player. Then roles are switched and the drill is flawlessly repeated as often as possible.

6. The player with the ball puts it between his feet and jumps. As he jumps, he jackknifes his body and passes the ball to the chest of his teammate. The teammate lets the ball bounce to the ground, puts it between his feet, and returns it the same way. Again the pass is repeated as often as possible without a miss by either partner.

"Playing one-on-one is the best conditioner I know of for improving both stamina and agility." Speaking, Andy Provan, 5-foot-5, 140-pound forward called The Flea when he played in England and later Philadelphia in the NASL.

"I gave him the name," says his former coach, Al Miller. "He could sometimes change directions 20 or 30 times while dribbling. His quick change of directions reminded me of a flea's movements."

A Sting player does another stretching exercise favored by the pros. He grips his knees alternately and touches his forehead to each knee.

At practice Miller set up goals about 30 yards apart for one-on-one drills. Provan dribbled toward the opposing goal and the defending player tried to take the ball away from him. If Provan dribbled around him, the player had to chase, but if the defender took the ball away from Provan, then Provan had to chase the player as he dribbled toward Provan's goal.

"In this situation both players are improving their agility," Al Miller once wrote in a book, *Winning Soccer*. And he added that "one versus one, with two goals approximately 30 yards apart, is one of the best practices I know for players from six to professional age."

Stamina, speed in getting to the ball, and agility are probably the three things soccer superstars need most. "To build my stamina," Kyle Rote, Jr., says, "I wore ankle weights when I ran laps around the field. I even wore them when I practiced my dribbling and my passing. I also wore ankle weights when I practiced my heading. When you take those weights off for a real game, your legs will feel as light as feathers. But the best way to build stamina is to run and run and run. Run one more lap than you did the day before. When I could, I even ran from the practice field to my house."

The foot race to the ball isn't always won by the fastest player. "You can win that race to the ball," says the Sting's Charlie Fajkus, "even if you might lose the 100-yard dash to your opponent. You have got to explode from a standing start and cover a distance of 15 to 20 feet as quickly as you can. It's what we call 'speed off the mark.' "

To build that speed off the mark the pros make this point: Cover those 15 to 20 feet with as few steps as possible. It is taking too many steps that consumes time and makes you slower off the mark than you should be.

Many pros suggest this conditioning drill to make you faster off the mark: Sprint the length of the penalty area and count the number of steps you took to cover those 18 yards. Then, after a rest,

Chicago Sting players go through limbering and stretching exercises before practice.

sprint the 18 yards again, concentrating on pushing off with your foot as you run, and stretching out your stride. Sprint the distance a third time and again count your steps. They should be fewer. Sprint the 18-yard distance every day, working to reduce the number of steps.

As for agility, the third physical element that soccer stars need, your agility will increase the more you play. The six agility drills mentioned earlier will help, as will drills players make up on their own during practice. In soccer as in anything else, practice is the first step toward greatness. Let's take a look at some of the greats of soccer—and see how they got to the top.

THE GREATEST

It isn't as famous as baseball's Hall of Fame in Cooperstown, New York, or pro football's Hall of Fame in Canton, Ohio. But there is a United States National Soccer Hall of Fame, located in Philadelphia. Among the greats honored there is an entire team—the 1950 United States World Cup team. Here's why:

America's Greatest Soccer Victory

Every four years the soccer-playing nations compete for the World Cup. This is the World Series of soccer. The winning team holds the Cup for the next four years and is saluted around the world as No. 1.

The United States has never won the World Cup. But on a rutted field in Brazil on June 27th, 1950, a team of Americans pulled off what is still considered the greatest upset in World Cup history.

The Americans were playing the English, who, the night before the game, had celebrated their triumph over Chile. After beating the swift and graceful South Americans, the English had no doubt they could beat the Americans, few of whom had ever played in world-class competition.

The American team was led by Joe Gaetjens, who had been born in Haiti but had developed his skills on the soccer fields of Brooklyn. One of his teammates, Walter Bahr, said of Joe: "He could kick balls into the net that no other player could even reach."

Early in the game an American took a shot at the English goalkeeper that went wide of the cage. Joe flew high into the air and headed the shot past the startled English goalkeeper. The Americans led the stunned English, 1-0.

The English never recovered, even though their fans kept shouting "Wake up!" from the stands. No one else scored and the Americans were 1-0 victors. They were defeated in a later round of Cup play, but their victory over the British, the founders of modern soccer, still causes English heads to bow in dismay. "How would you like it," an English soccer player once said to an American, "if we sent an English baseball team to the States and that team beat the Yankees in the World Series?"

Joe Gaetjens and Walter Bahr are enshrined in the U.S. National Soccer Hall of Fame as members of that World Cup team. But Walter Bahr could be there for another reason apart from that 1950 upset.

The Greatest Family of American Soccer

Walter Bahr became the soccer coach at Penn State after that 1950 Cup victory. His oldest son, Casey, played for the 1972

U.S. Olympic soccer team. Another son, Chris, was a soccer All-American at Penn State, a midfielder for the NASL team in Philadelphia, and was picked as the 1975 NASL Rookie of the Year. But he achieved greater fame as a field-goal kicker for the NFL Oakland Raiders, the 1981 Super Bowl champs. Another Bahr son, Matt, was also an All-American soccer player at Penn State, and a member of the NASL Colorado and Tulsa teams. But, like his brother, he attained greater fame kicking field goals—for the Super Bowl champion Pittsburgh Steelers.

If the greatest players and events of soccer, both in the United States and around the world, were to be immortalized in the Hall of Fame in Philadelphia, these people and these events would deserve a place there.

The Greatest Scorer

Pelé. From September 7, 1956, to October 2, 1974, he scored 1,216 goals, almost one per game for Santos, his Brazilian team.

When he scored his 1,000th goal, a writer made this point:

"That 1,000th goal was perhaps the most astonishing record in sports. It was even greater than Hank Aaron's 715th homer that broke Babe Ruth's record of 714. To understand why, remember this: When Pelé scored his 1,000th goal, the nearest to him of any player in the world was another Brazilian. He had 550."

Pelé scored that 1,000th goal on November 19, 1969, before almost 100,000 fans in a Rio de Janeiro stadium. It came on a penalty kick and when the ball shook the nets, radio broadcasters across South America broke into programs with a news flash that caused people to dance in the streets: *The great Pelé has scored number one thousand!*

The Greatest U.S. College Team

For sheer winning, the Penn State team of 1932 to 1941 wins hands down. Coached by Scottish-born Bill Jeffrey, later the coach of the 1950 U.S. World Cup team, the soccer Nittany Lions were unbeaten in 65 straight games.

The Greatest Save

He has seen many goals and many saves,

so Pelé speaks with authority when he says: "That was the greatest save I have ever seen."

It took place during the 1970 World Cup game between England and Brazil, played in Mexico. A Brazilian, Jairzinho, sped down the right sideline and booted a high crossing pass that bounded in front of the unprotected goal, and its keeper, baggy-eyed Gordon Banks. He watched Pelé rise into the air to meet the bounding ball.

"Pelé came up like a salmon," Banks later recalled. "With those tremendous neck muscles, he hit a tremendous header. It was the most dangerous kind, just short of the goal line, hit so that it would bounce up and in."

Banks had been standing on the far side of the cage to block the shot from Jairzinho. Seeing the crossing pass to Pelé, he dashed to the middle of the cage. But it looked like he had "missed the bus." Pelé, corkscrewing into the air, had already nodded that header on a bounce toward the far corner of the cage.

Banks left his feet with a tremendous leap. As he knifed through the air, he saw the ball below him bounce just short of the goal line. It floated up toward him and he stretched out his right hand to the level he thought the ball would reach on the final bounce. His right hand reached the ball and ticked it upward. The ball flew harmlessly over the cage.

Pelé had already spun around, hands high into the air, celebrating the goal. Then his mouth dropped in dismay. The goal had not scored and Gordon Banks had made "the greatest save."

The Greatest Scorer
(United States Division)

Giorgio Chinaglia is the greatest scorer in the history of North American soccer. Born in Italy and raised in England, he is now a U.S. citizen. For three years, 1979, 1980, and 1981, he led the North American Soccer League in scoring. By the end of the 1981 season he was the all-time NASL scoring champion with more than 150 goals.

"Scoring goals,' he once said, "that is what soccer is all about. If you don't shoot, you don't score. And if you don't score, you don't win."

When Pelé joined the Cosmos, he asked Giorgio why he took so many shots from bad angles. "For Chinaglia,"

Giorgio said grandly, "there are no bad angles."

Chinaglia was at his deadliest in the 1980 playoffs. In a game against Tulsa, he took a pass from a teammate and booted the ball into the cage for the Cosmos' first goal. Minutes later he scored again on a penalty kick. Then he rammed home another ball on a penalty kick. His three goals had put the Cosmos ahead, 3-0. He received passes from teammates to kick home goals No. 4, 5, 6, and 7. The Cosmos won, 8-1 and Chinaglia's seven goals in one game were a U.S. pro soccer record. It is one of almost a dozen records owned by Chinaglia. In the 1980 playoffs he also scored 18 of his team's total of 25 goals, another NASL record. "He's awkward, he's clumsy, he hangs around the penalty area," former NASL coach Hubert Vogelsinger once said of Chinaglia. "And just when you're laughing at him, he sticks the ball in the back of the net."

SUPER ATHLETES
QUIZ

This chapter will tell you: **1.** how smart a player you are; and **2.** how expert a fan you are.

The quiz for players will determine if your head is as good as your feet should be. There are 20 questions. A score of 15 or higher puts you in the starting lineup. From 10 to 14 puts you on the bench, almost ready for full-time duty. Nine or below? You are still a rookie.

The second quiz will test how knowing a fan you are. It also has 20 questions. A score of 15 or higher puts you in the press box with the experts. A score of 10 to 14 seats you in the grandstands as an ordinary fan. If you score nine or below, you need to see a few more soccer games.

Take both tests, then check your answers at the end of the chapter.

QUIZ FOR PLAYERS

1. When a coach says to "cross" the ball, he means you should
   a. put an X on the ball.
   b. dribble the ball across the field
   c. pass the ball from one corner across the field into the penalty area.
2. When you "volley" the ball, you
   a. aim it at an opponent.
   b. kick the ball as hard as you can.
   c. kick the ball while it is in flight.
3. A wall pass is one that you
   a. bounce off a wall of defenders.
   b. pass to a teammate, who then passes it back to you as you go around an opponent
   c. bounce off a handball wall.

4. If you are a striker, you should concentrate on
   a. getting the players to strike against the coach.
   b. passing.
   c. scoring.
5. If you are a sweeper, you
   a. are the defender who looks to intercept passes near the goal line.
   b. are the team's janitor.
   c. are the attacker who sweeps the ball toward the opposing goal.
6. When you are "heading" a ball, you should strike it with
   a. the forehead.
   b. the top of the head.
   c. the back of the head.
7. When you, as a goalkeeper, "distribute" a ball to teammates after stopping a shot, you can
   a. kick the ball to them.
   b. roll the ball to them.
   c. do both.
8. When you are marking an opponent, try to stand
   a. next to him.
   b. in front of him.
   c. behind him.

9. The most accurate short passes are delivered off
   a. the inside of the foot.
   b. the toes.
   c. the part of the shoe where the laces are.
10. In booting a ball from within 12 feet of the goal, you should kick the ball
    a. with the toe of the foot.
    b. on the side of the big toe.
    c. on the instep.
11. In soccer it is permissible to bump or jar an opponent who has the ball with the shoulders but not the arms, hands, elbows, or hips.
    a. True
    b. False
    c. Sometimes
12. In tackling an opponent to take the ball away from him or her, you can hit the opponent's legs.
    a. True
    b. False
    c. Sometimes
13. As an attacking midfielder or forward, you should try to move the ball
    a. down the middle of the field.
    b. down the sideline.
    c. back and forth across the middle of the field.

14. When you are dribbling, the faster you run   .
  a. the farther the ball should be kicked on each touch.
  b. the closer to you the ball should be kicked.
  c. the more cockeyed it should be kicked.

15. When a pass is coming toward you, you should
  a. wait for the ball.
  b. move away from the ball.
  c. move toward the ball.

16. When dribbling with the ball, keep your head
  a. down.
  b. up.
  c. moving down and up and sideways.

17. On a penalty shot, the kicker should hit the ball
  a. low and to the corner.
  b. high and to the corner.
  c. straight at the keeper.

18. When the ball is bouncing around the cage, a goalkeeper should
  a. shout directions and instructions to defenders.
  b. shout only to the team captain.
  c. keep his mouth shut.

19. In leaping to stop a shot, the goal-keeper should
    a. spring from one foot.
    b. spring with both feet.
    c. spring with both hands.
20. You are the goalkeeper and an attacker is coming at you with the ball from the right side. You should
    a. come out moving toward your right side.
    b. come out moving toward your left side.
    c. come out quickly and fall down.

QUIZ FOR FANS

1. Which nation has won the World Cup three times?
   a. Italy
   b. Brazil
   c. England
2. Which NASL team has participated in the most playoff games?
   a. New York
   b. Seattle
   c. Fort Lauderdale
3. How fast does a soccer ball travel when kicked by a pro like George Best or Pelé?
   a. 40 mph   b. 50 mph   c. 60 mph

4. What is the width and height of an official NASL goal?
   a. 10 yards wide and 10 feet high
   b. 8 yards wide and 8 feet high
   c. 6 yards wide and 6 feet high
5. The "pitch" in soccer is
   a. the field
   b. the throw of a goalkeeper to a teammate.
   c. a pass from out of bounds.
6. A yellow card is held up by an official to warn a player that
   a. the player has committed a major foul.
   b. the player is playing in a cowardly fashion.
   c. the player is in the wrong area of the field.
7. A player is called for being offside if there are
   a. fewer than three defenders between the player and the goal when the ball is passed by his or her team.
   b. fewer than two defenders between the player and the goal.
   c. one defender between the player and the goal.

8. A banana kick is
   a. a bad one.
   b. one used by South American players from banana-exporting countries.
   c. one that curves.
9. The numbers in a formation like a 4-3-3 refer, in this order, to
   a. forwards, midfielders, defenders.
   b. midfielders, defenders, forwards.
   c. defenders, midfielders, forwards.
10. The World Cup competition is held
    a. every year.
    b. every four years.
    c. every Olympic year.
11. A player commits two fouls at the same time. He is penalized for
    a. the less serious one.
    b. neither.
    c. the more serious one.
12. If a ball bursts during a game, a new ball should
    a. be thrown in from the sideline.
    b. be thrown in by the goalkeeper who last handled the ball.
    c. be dropped at the point where the original ball burst.

13. In his career Pelé scored more than
    a. 1,000 goals.
    b. 700 goals.
    c. 500 goals.
14. When a player half-volleys, he or she
    a. drop-kicks the ball just as it bounces off the ground.
    b. cuts a volley in half.
    c. catches a volley in mid-air.
15. What is the weight of an official pro soccer ball?
    a. 10 to 12 ounces
    b. 6 to 8 ounces
    c. 14 to 16 ounces
16. The penalty area is
    a. 12 yards deep.
    b. 14 yards deep.
    c. 18 yards deep.
17. When a player throws in a ball that has gone out of bounds, he or she must have
    a. both feet on the ground.
    b. at least one foot on the ground.
    c. no feet on the ground.

18. When a coach says a player "over-lapped," he means
    a. one defender went into offensive territory.
    b. a player drank too much water.
    c. a player is exhausted.
19. Which of these three top players was not American-born?
    a. Giorgio Chinaglia
    b. Jim McAlister
    c. Shep Messing
20. Which is the oldest soccer league in the United States?
    a. American Soccer League
    b. North American Soccer League
    c. Neither

ANSWERS

Quiz for Players

1. c.	11. a.
2. c.	12. b.
3. b.	13. a.
4. c.	14. a.
5. a.	15. c.
6. a.	16. c.
7. c.	17. a.
8. c.	18. a.
9. a.	19. a.
10. b.	20. a

Quiz for Fans

1. b.	11. c.
2. a.	12. c.
3. c.	13. a.
4. b.	14. a.
5. a.	15. c.
6. a.	16. c.
7. b.	17. a.
8. c.	18. a.
9. c.	19. a.
10. b.	20. a.

THE
SECRETS LIST

Bet these are things you didn't know about soccer, even if you have read the *Guinness Book of World Records:*

How Pelé Got His Name: Even as a little boy in Brazil, Edison Arantes do Nascimento was called Pelé. Many have said that he got the name from playing *peladas*, a Portuguese word for sandlot soccer games. From *peladas*, according to legend, came the nickname that is now world famous: Pelé.

But in the summer of 1981, Pelé told a boy in East Hampton, New York, this story: In Portuguese *Pe* is short for foot, and *le* is short for lazy. When Pelé was a boy some of his friends teased that he had a lazy or slow foot when he kicked the ball. "And so," he told the boy, "they began to call me Pelé."

From Goals to Homers: Two of baseball's greatest players were also soccer stars as boys. Babe Ruth was a goalkeeper for the St. Mary's School for Boys in Baltimore. And Lou Gehrig was a defender for his New York City high school team.

My Dad, the Coach: Keith Furphey was one of the star players for the Detroit Express in 1978. The team was coached by his father, Keith Furphey.

Brothers and Keepers: During the 1979 season, the Rochester Lancers had two goalkeepers. One was named Shep and the other Ray, and both were Messings. They were brothers.

Family Affairs: One of the few husband-and-wife teams in soccer was Debbie and Charlie Fejkus. Charlie was a midfielder for the Chicago Sting, while Debbie was a sweeper for the Wheaton Rebels.

Most Surprised Mother: When Cosmos rookie Chico Borja scored a goal in his first game, his mother—watching in the stands—fainted.

Soccer's Knight: One of the great English players from 1930 to the mid-1950s was Stanley Matthews. He was never paid more than about $60 a week, but in 1955 he got an extraordinary reward. Queen Elizabeth made him a knight.

Best "Homers": Brazil's Fluminese team didn't lose a game at home from 1957 to 1980.

Quickest Scorer: The earliest goal ever scored in an NASL game was registered by Seattle's Derek Smethurst. He put the ball into the net 11 seconds after the game began.

What's in a Name? Soccer is called *football* or a variation of that name almost everywhere in the world except the United States, Canada, and Australia. No one knows why, but the ruling body of soccer in England is the Football Association and the word "association" may have been shortened to "soccer."

If you liked SECRETS OF THE SUPER ATHLETES: **Soccer**, don't miss the other books in this series:

★ Football by Abbot Neil Solomon
★ Basketball by David Fremon
★ Baseball by Abbot Neil Solomon

Get the inside line on the most popular sports in America today—straight talk and secret tips from the greatest players, the professional viewpoint from the coaches and managers of the champion teams, plus more action and more hard information than you can find in any other sports books.

All four books are packed with action photos of your favorite stars.

Be an all-round winner, a sports fan who knows what he's talking about, a player who knows how to win. Buy the entire series of SECRETS OF THE SUPER ATHLETES.